50 Filipino Recipes for Home

By: Kelly Johnson

Table of Contents

- Chicken Adobo
- Sinigang na Baboy (Pork Sour Soup)
- Pancit Canton (Stir-Fried Noodles)
- Lumpiang Shanghai (Filipino Spring Rolls)
- Kare-Kare (Oxtail Stew in Peanut Sauce)
- Lechon Kawali (Crispy Fried Pork Belly)
- Chicken Tinola (Ginger Chicken Soup)
- Beef Mechado (Braised Beef in Tomato Sauce)
- Pork Sinigang (Pork Sour Soup)
- Beef Caldereta (Filipino Beef Stew)
- Pork Binagoongan (Pork in Shrimp Paste)
- Ginataang Kalabasa at Sitaw (Squash and String Beans in Coconut Milk)
- Tortang Talong (Eggplant Omelette)
- Beef Kare-Kare (Beef Stew in Peanut Sauce)
- Ginataang Hipon (Shrimp in Coconut Milk)
- Chicken Afritada (Chicken Stewed in Tomato Sauce)
- Sisig (Sizzling Pork or Chicken)
- Pinakbet (Mixed Vegetables in Shrimp Paste)
- Laing (Taro Leaves in Coconut Milk)
- Pork Adobo Flakes
- Ginisang Upo (Sauteed Bottle Gourd)
- Bangus (Milkfish) Belly Paksiw
- Ginataang Langka (Young Jackfruit in Coconut Milk)
- Ginisang Sayote (Sauteed Chayote)
- Bicol Express (Spicy Pork in Coconut Milk)
- Beef Sinigang (Beef Sour Soup)
- Chicken Tinola sa Papaya (Chicken Soup with Papaya)
- Pininyahang Manok (Chicken with Pineapple)
- Dinuguan (Pork Blood Stew)
- Ginisang Ampalaya (Sauteed Bitter Melon)
- Inihaw na Liempo (Grilled Pork Belly)
- Binakol (Chicken Soup with Coconut Water)
- Kilawin (Filipino Ceviche)
- Ginisang Monggo (Mung Bean Soup)
- Ginisang Labanos (Sauteed Radish)

- Balut (Fertilized Duck Egg)
- Kinilaw na Isda (Fish Ceviche)
- Pochero (Filipino Beef Stew)
- Rellenong Bangus (Stuffed Milkfish)
- Sinampalukang Manok (Chicken Tamarind Soup)
- Adobong Pusit (Squid Adobo)
- Kare-Kareng Gulay (Vegetable Stew in Peanut Sauce)
- Ukoy (Shrimp Fritters)
- Pancit Bihon (Rice Noodles)
- Gising-Gising (Spicy Green Beans in Coconut Milk)
- Ensaladang Talong (Eggplant Salad)
- Pork Menudo (Pork Stew)
- Chicken Inasal (Grilled Chicken)
- Tinolang Tahong (Mussels Soup with Ginger)
- Ginataang Manok (Chicken in Coconut Milk)

Chicken Adobo

Ingredients:

- 2 lbs (about 900g) chicken thighs, bone-in and skin-on, cut into serving pieces
- 1/2 cup soy sauce
- 1/2 cup white vinegar
- 1 cup water
- 4 cloves garlic, minced
- 1 onion, sliced
- 3 bay leaves
- 1 teaspoon whole black peppercorns
- 2 tablespoons cooking oil
- Salt and pepper to taste
- Optional: sliced green onions for garnish

Instructions:

1. In a large bowl, combine the soy sauce, white vinegar, water, minced garlic, sliced onion, bay leaves, and whole black peppercorns. Mix well.
2. Add the chicken pieces to the marinade, making sure they are well coated. Cover the bowl and marinate the chicken in the refrigerator for at least 1 hour, or overnight for best flavor.
3. Heat the cooking oil in a large skillet or pot over medium-high heat. Remove the chicken pieces from the marinade (reserving the marinade) and add them to the hot skillet, skin side down. Brown the chicken pieces on both sides, about 5 minutes per side. You may need to do this in batches to avoid overcrowding the pan.
4. Once the chicken is browned, add the reserved marinade to the skillet. Bring the mixture to a boil, then reduce the heat to low. Cover and simmer for about 30-40 minutes, or until the chicken is tender and fully cooked, stirring occasionally.
5. Once the chicken is cooked through, uncover the skillet and increase the heat to medium-high. Allow the sauce to reduce and thicken slightly, about 10-15 minutes, stirring occasionally.
6. Taste the sauce and adjust the seasoning with salt and pepper if needed.
7. Once the sauce has reached your desired consistency and the chicken is fully cooked, remove the skillet from the heat.

8. Transfer the Chicken Adobo to a serving platter and garnish with sliced green onions, if desired.
9. Serve the Chicken Adobo hot with steamed rice and your favorite vegetable side dish.

Enjoy the delicious flavors of this classic Filipino dish! Adjust the seasoning and ingredients according to your taste preferences.

Sinigang na Baboy (Pork Sour Soup)

Ingredients:

- 1 lb (about 450g) pork belly or pork ribs, cut into serving pieces
- 8 cups water
- 1 medium onion, quartered
- 2 tomatoes, quartered
- 2 cups sliced daikon radish
- 1 cup sliced eggplant
- 1 cup green beans, trimmed and cut into 2-inch pieces
- 2 cups spinach leaves or kangkong (water spinach)
- 3 tablespoons tamarind soup base or tamarind powder
- Salt or fish sauce (patis) to taste
- Optional: sliced green chili peppers for extra heat
- Optional: calamansi or lime wedges for serving

Instructions:

1. In a large pot, combine the water and pork pieces. Bring to a boil over medium-high heat, skimming off any foam that rises to the surface.
2. Once boiling, add the quartered onion and tomatoes to the pot. Cover and simmer for about 30-40 minutes, or until the pork is tender.
3. Add the sliced daikon radish to the pot and simmer for an additional 5 minutes.
4. Stir in the sliced eggplant and green beans, and continue to simmer for another 5 minutes, or until the vegetables are tender.
5. Add the tamarind soup base or tamarind powder to the pot, stirring to dissolve. Taste the soup and adjust the sourness by adding more tamarind if desired.
6. Season the Sinigang na Baboy with salt or fish sauce to taste. If you like your sinigang spicier, you can also add sliced green chili peppers at this point.
7. Add the spinach leaves or kangkong to the pot and cook for a couple of minutes until wilted.
8. Remove the pot from the heat and serve the Sinigang na Baboy hot with steamed rice. You can also serve it with calamansi or lime wedges on the side for squeezing over the soup.
9. Enjoy the tangy and savory flavors of this comforting Filipino dish!

Sinigang na Baboy is often enjoyed as a main course for lunch or dinner, especially on rainy days or cold evenings. Adjust the ingredients and seasonings according to your taste preferences.

Pancit Canton (Stir-Fried Noodles)

Ingredients:

- 1/2 lb (about 225g) pancit canton noodles (or any wheat noodles)
- 2 tablespoons cooking oil
- 4 cloves garlic, minced
- 1 onion, sliced
- 1/2 lb (about 225g) boneless chicken breast or thigh, thinly sliced
- 1/2 lb (about 225g) shrimp, peeled and deveined
- 1 cup sliced cabbage
- 1 medium carrot, julienned
- 1 bell pepper, sliced
- 1 cup sliced snow peas or snap peas
- 1/4 cup soy sauce
- 2 tablespoons oyster sauce
- 1 tablespoon fish sauce
- 1 teaspoon sugar
- Salt and pepper to taste
- Calamansi or lemon wedges, for serving
- Optional garnishes: chopped green onions, fried garlic, hard-boiled eggs

Instructions:

1. Cook the pancit canton noodles according to package instructions until they are al dente. Drain and set aside.
2. In a large wok or skillet, heat the cooking oil over medium-high heat. Add the minced garlic and sliced onion, and sauté until fragrant and translucent.
3. Add the thinly sliced chicken to the wok and stir-fry until it is cooked through and no longer pink.
4. Push the chicken to one side of the wok and add the peeled and deveined shrimp. Cook until the shrimp turns pink and opaque.
5. Stir in the sliced vegetables (cabbage, carrot, bell pepper, and snow peas) and cook until they are tender-crisp.
6. Add the cooked pancit canton noodles to the wok, along with the soy sauce, oyster sauce, fish sauce, and sugar. Toss everything together until the noodles and ingredients are well combined and evenly coated with the sauce.

7. Taste the pancit canton and adjust the seasoning with salt and pepper if needed.
8. Remove the wok from the heat and transfer the pancit canton to a serving platter.
9. Garnish the pancit canton with chopped green onions, fried garlic, and sliced hard-boiled eggs if desired.
10. Serve the pancit canton hot, with calamansi or lemon wedges on the side for squeezing over the noodles.
11. Enjoy this delicious and comforting Filipino stir-fried noodle dish!

Feel free to customize this pancit canton recipe by adding your favorite vegetables or protein options such as pork, beef, or tofu. Adjust the seasonings according to your taste preferences.

Lumpiang Shanghai (Filipino Spring Rolls)

Ingredients:

- 1 lb (about 450g) ground pork or beef
- 1 medium carrot, grated
- 1 small onion, finely chopped
- 2 cloves garlic, minced
- 1/2 cup green onions, chopped
- 1/2 cup finely chopped cabbage
- 1 egg
- 1 tablespoon soy sauce
- 1 teaspoon salt
- 1/2 teaspoon black pepper
- Lumpia or spring roll wrappers (about 25-30 pieces)
- Cooking oil for frying
- Sweet chili sauce or banana ketchup, for dipping (optional)

Instructions:

1. In a large bowl, combine the ground pork or beef, grated carrot, chopped onion, minced garlic, chopped green onions, chopped cabbage, egg, soy sauce, salt, and black pepper. Mix well until all the ingredients are evenly distributed.
2. Lay a lumpia wrapper on a clean, dry surface, with one corner facing you (like a diamond shape).
3. Spoon about 1 to 2 tablespoons of the meat mixture onto the bottom third of the wrapper, spreading it into a log shape.
4. Fold the bottom corner of the wrapper over the filling, then fold in the sides to enclose the filling completely. Roll the wrapper tightly away from you, sealing the edge with a little water. Repeat with the remaining wrappers and filling.
5. Heat cooking oil in a deep skillet or frying pan over medium heat. Once the oil is hot, carefully add the lumpiang Shanghai in batches, seam side down, and fry until golden brown and crispy, about 3-5 minutes per side.
6. Use tongs to carefully turn the lumpiang Shanghai to ensure even frying. Remove from the oil and drain on paper towels to remove excess oil.
7. Serve the lumpiang Shanghai hot, with sweet chili sauce or banana ketchup for dipping, if desired.

8. Enjoy these delicious Filipino spring rolls as an appetizer or snack!

Lumpiang Shanghai can also be made ahead of time and frozen before frying. To cook from frozen, fry the lumpia straight from the freezer, adding a few extra minutes to the frying time.

Kare-Kare (Oxtail Stew in Peanut Sauce)

Ingredients:

- 2 lbs (about 900g) oxtail, cut into 2-inch pieces
- 1 lb (about 450g) beef tripe, cleaned and sliced (optional)
- 1 large eggplant, sliced
- 1 bunch Chinese long beans (sitaw) or green beans, cut into 2-inch pieces
- 1 medium banana blossom (puso ng saging), sliced (optional)
- 1/2 cup peanut butter
- 2 tablespoons annatto seeds (achuete)
- 1 medium onion, chopped
- 4 cloves garlic, minced
- 6 cups beef broth or water
- 2 tablespoons cooking oil
- Salt and pepper to taste
- Shrimp paste (bagoong) for serving (optional)

Instructions:

1. In a large pot, heat the cooking oil over medium heat. Add the annatto seeds and cook until the oil turns red and becomes infused with color. Remove the seeds and discard.
2. Sauté the chopped onion and minced garlic in the annatto oil until softened and aromatic.
3. Add the oxtail pieces and beef tripe (if using) to the pot. Cook until they are browned on all sides.
4. Pour in the beef broth or water, making sure the meat is submerged. Bring to a boil, then reduce the heat to low. Cover and simmer for about 2 to 3 hours, or until the oxtail and tripe are tender. You can also use a pressure cooker to speed up the cooking time.
5. Once the meat is tender, add the eggplant slices, Chinese long beans, and banana blossom (if using) to the pot. Continue to simmer until the vegetables are cooked through, about 10 to 15 minutes.
6. In a small bowl, mix the peanut butter with a ladle of the hot broth from the pot until smooth and creamy. Stir the peanut butter mixture into the stew until well incorporated. Season with salt and pepper to taste.

7. Continue to simmer the Kare-Kare for a few more minutes to thicken the sauce and allow the flavors to meld together.
8. Remove the pot from the heat and transfer the Kare-Kare to a serving dish.
9. Serve the Kare-Kare hot, accompanied by shrimp paste (bagoong) on the side for dipping, if desired.
10. Enjoy this delicious and comforting Filipino stew with steamed rice!

Kare-Kare is often served at special occasions and gatherings, and it's best enjoyed with a side of shrimp paste for added flavor. Adjust the ingredients and seasonings according to your taste preferences.

Lechon Kawali (Crispy Fried Pork Belly)

Ingredients:

- 2 lbs (about 900g) pork belly, skin-on
- 1 tablespoon salt
- 1 teaspoon black peppercorns
- 4 cloves garlic, crushed
- 3 bay leaves
- Water for boiling
- Cooking oil for deep frying

Instructions:

1. In a large pot, combine the pork belly, salt, black peppercorns, crushed garlic, and bay leaves. Add enough water to cover the pork belly.
2. Bring the water to a boil over medium-high heat, then reduce the heat to low. Cover the pot and simmer the pork belly for about 45 minutes to 1 hour, or until the meat is tender.
3. Once the pork belly is tender, remove it from the pot and let it cool slightly. You can also refrigerate it for a few hours or overnight to allow the skin to dry out, which will help achieve a crispier texture when frying.
4. Heat cooking oil in a deep fryer or a large, heavy-bottomed pot to 350°F (175°C).
5. Carefully add the pork belly to the hot oil, skin side down. Be cautious, as the oil may splatter.
6. Fry the pork belly for about 8-10 minutes, or until the skin is golden brown and crispy. Use tongs to turn the pork belly occasionally for even frying.
7. Once the skin is crispy, flip the pork belly over and continue frying for another 8-10 minutes, or until the meat is fully cooked and golden brown all over.
8. Remove the crispy fried pork belly from the oil and drain it on paper towels to remove excess oil.
9. Let the Lechon Kawali rest for a few minutes before slicing it into serving pieces.
10. Serve the Lechon Kawali hot, with your favorite dipping sauce such as vinegar with garlic and chili, or soy sauce with calamansi.
11. Enjoy the delicious and crispy goodness of this Filipino favorite!

Lechon Kawali is often served with steamed rice and a side of vegetables or pickled relish. Adjust the seasoning and cooking time according to your taste preferences.

Chicken Tinola (Ginger Chicken Soup)

Ingredients:

- 1 whole chicken, cut into serving pieces
- 1 tablespoon cooking oil
- 1 thumb-sized piece of ginger, peeled and sliced into thin strips
- 3 cloves garlic, minced
- 1 onion, chopped
- 2-3 cups water or chicken broth
- 1 green papaya or chayote squash, peeled and cut into wedges
- 2 cups spinach leaves or chili leaves (dahon ng sili)
- Fish sauce (patis) or salt, to taste
- Ground black pepper, to taste
- Optional garnish: chopped green onions or cilantro

Instructions:

1. In a large pot, heat the cooking oil over medium heat. Add the sliced ginger, minced garlic, and chopped onion. Sauté until fragrant and the onions are translucent.
2. Add the chicken pieces to the pot and cook until lightly browned on all sides.
3. Pour in the water or chicken broth, making sure the chicken is fully submerged. Bring to a boil, then reduce the heat to low and let it simmer for about 20-30 minutes, or until the chicken is tender.
4. Once the chicken is tender, add the green papaya or chayote squash wedges to the pot. Simmer for an additional 8-10 minutes, or until the vegetables are cooked but still firm.
5. Season the soup with fish sauce or salt and ground black pepper to taste. Adjust the seasoning according to your preference.
6. Add the spinach leaves or chili leaves to the pot and cook for a couple of minutes until wilted.
7. Remove the pot from the heat and transfer the Chicken Tinola to a serving bowl.
8. Garnish with chopped green onions or cilantro, if desired.
9. Serve the Chicken Tinola hot with steamed rice on the side.
10. Enjoy this comforting and nutritious Ginger Chicken Soup!

Feel free to adjust the ingredients and seasoning according to your taste preferences.

Beef Mechado (Braised Beef in Tomato Sauce)

Ingredients:

- 2 lbs (about 900g) beef chuck or round roast, cut into large chunks
- 2 tablespoons cooking oil
- 1 onion, chopped
- 4 cloves garlic, minced
- 2 tomatoes, chopped
- 3 tablespoons tomato paste
- 2 cups beef broth
- 1 bay leaf
- 2 tablespoons soy sauce
- 2 tablespoons calamansi juice or lemon juice
- 1 large carrot, sliced
- 2 potatoes, peeled and quartered
- Salt and pepper to taste
- Optional garnish: chopped green onions or cilantro

Instructions:

1. Heat the cooking oil in a large pot or Dutch oven over medium heat. Add the chopped onion and minced garlic, sautéing until they turn translucent and fragrant.
2. Add the beef chunks to the pot and cook until browned on all sides, about 5-7 minutes.
3. Stir in the chopped tomatoes and tomato paste, cooking for an additional 2-3 minutes.
4. Pour in the beef broth and add the bay leaf, soy sauce, and calamansi juice (or lemon juice). Bring the mixture to a boil, then reduce the heat to low. Cover and simmer for about 1.5 to 2 hours, or until the beef is tender.
5. Once the beef is tender, add the sliced carrot and quartered potatoes to the pot. Continue to simmer for an additional 20-30 minutes, or until the vegetables are cooked through.
6. Season the Beef Mechado with salt and pepper to taste.
7. Remove the bay leaf from the pot and discard it.

8. Transfer the Beef Mechado to a serving dish and garnish with chopped green onions or cilantro, if desired.
9. Serve the Beef Mechado hot with steamed rice on the side.
10. Enjoy the rich flavors of this hearty Filipino braised beef dish!

Feel free to adjust the ingredients and seasonings according to your preferences. Beef Mechado is a comforting meal perfect for family gatherings and special occasions.

Pork Sinigang (Pork Sour Soup)

Ingredients:

- 1 lb (about 450g) pork belly or pork ribs, cut into serving pieces
- 8 cups water
- 1 medium onion, quartered
- 2 tomatoes, quartered
- 2 cups sliced daikon radish
- 1 cup sliced eggplant
- 1 cup green beans, trimmed and cut into 2-inch pieces
- 2 cups spinach leaves or kangkong (water spinach)
- 3 tablespoons tamarind soup base or tamarind powder
- Salt or fish sauce (patis) to taste
- Optional: sliced green chili peppers for extra heat
- Optional: calamansi or lime wedges for serving

Instructions:

1. In a large pot, combine the water, pork pieces, onion, and tomatoes. Bring to a boil over medium-high heat, then reduce the heat to low. Cover and simmer for about 45 minutes to 1 hour, or until the pork is tender.
2. Once the pork is tender, add the sliced daikon radish to the pot and simmer for an additional 5 minutes.
3. Stir in the sliced eggplant and green beans, and continue to simmer for another 5 minutes, or until the vegetables are tender.
4. Add the tamarind soup base or tamarind powder to the pot, stirring to dissolve. Taste the soup and adjust the sourness by adding more tamarind if desired.
5. Season the sinigang with salt or fish sauce to taste. If you like your sinigang spicier, you can also add sliced green chili peppers at this point.
6. Add the spinach leaves or kangkong to the pot and cook for a couple of minutes until wilted.
7. Remove the pot from the heat and serve the Pork Sinigang hot.
8. Serve the Pork Sinigang hot, with steamed rice on the side. You can also serve it with calamansi or lime wedges for squeezing over the soup.
9. Enjoy the tangy and savory flavors of this classic Filipino soup!

Feel free to adjust the ingredients and seasonings according to your taste preferences.

Pork Sinigang is a comforting and satisfying dish that is perfect for any occasion.

Beef Caldereta (Filipino Beef Stew)

Ingredients:

- 2 lbs (about 900g) beef stew meat, cut into cubes
- 2 tablespoons cooking oil
- 1 onion, chopped
- 4 cloves garlic, minced
- 2 tomatoes, chopped
- 3 tablespoons tomato paste
- 3 cups beef broth
- 1 cup tomato sauce
- 2 bay leaves
- 1 red bell pepper, sliced
- 1 green bell pepper, sliced
- 2 large potatoes, peeled and cubed
- 2 carrots, peeled and sliced
- 1/2 cup green peas (fresh or frozen)
- 1/4 cup liver spread or liver pate (optional)
- Salt and pepper to taste
- 1/4 cup grated cheese (optional, for garnish)
- Optional garnish: chopped green onions or cilantro

Instructions:

1. In a large pot or Dutch oven, heat the cooking oil over medium heat. Add the chopped onion and minced garlic, sautéing until they turn translucent and fragrant.
2. Add the beef cubes to the pot and cook until browned on all sides, about 5-7 minutes.
3. Stir in the chopped tomatoes and tomato paste, cooking for an additional 2-3 minutes.
4. Pour in the beef broth and tomato sauce, and add the bay leaves. Bring the mixture to a boil, then reduce the heat to low. Cover and simmer for about 1.5 to 2 hours, or until the beef is tender.

5. Once the beef is tender, add the sliced bell peppers, cubed potatoes, sliced carrots, and green peas to the pot. Simmer for an additional 20-30 minutes, or until the vegetables are cooked through.
6. Stir in the liver spread or liver pate (if using) to add richness and depth of flavor to the stew.
7. Season the Beef Caldereta with salt and pepper to taste.
8. Remove the bay leaves from the pot and discard them.
9. Transfer the Beef Caldereta to a serving dish and garnish with grated cheese and chopped green onions or cilantro, if desired.
10. Serve the Beef Caldereta hot with steamed rice on the side.
11. Enjoy the delicious and comforting flavors of this Filipino beef stew!

Beef Caldereta is a popular dish often served at family gatherings and special occasions. Feel free to adjust the ingredients and seasonings according to your preferences.

Pork Binagoongan (Pork in Shrimp Paste)

Ingredients:

- 1 lb (about 450g) pork belly, diced
- 3 tablespoons shrimp paste (bagoong)
- 2 tablespoons cooking oil
- 1 onion, chopped
- 4 cloves garlic, minced
- 2 tomatoes, diced
- 2 chili peppers (siling labuyo), chopped (optional for added heat)
- 1/4 cup vinegar
- 1 tablespoon sugar
- Salt and pepper to taste
- Water, as needed
- Optional garnish: chopped green onions or cilantro

Instructions:

1. Heat the cooking oil in a large skillet or wok over medium heat.
2. Add the diced pork belly to the skillet and cook until browned on all sides, about 5-7 minutes. Remove the pork from the skillet and set aside.
3. In the same skillet, add the chopped onion and minced garlic. Sauté until the onions become translucent and fragrant.
4. Add the diced tomatoes and chili peppers (if using) to the skillet. Cook until the tomatoes soften and release their juices.
5. Stir in the shrimp paste (bagoong) and cook for 2-3 minutes, allowing the flavors to meld together.
6. Return the browned pork to the skillet. Pour in the vinegar and add the sugar. Season with salt and pepper to taste.
7. Add enough water to cover the pork, then bring the mixture to a boil. Reduce the heat to low, cover, and simmer for about 30-40 minutes, or until the pork is tender and the sauce thickens.
8. Taste and adjust the seasoning if needed, adding more salt, pepper, or sugar according to your preference.
9. Once the pork is tender and the sauce has reached your desired consistency, remove the skillet from the heat.

10. Transfer the Pork Binagoongan to a serving dish and garnish with chopped green onions or cilantro, if desired.
11. Serve the Pork Binagoongan hot with steamed rice on the side.
12. Enjoy the rich and savory flavors of this classic Filipino dish!

Feel free to adjust the spiciness by adding more or fewer chili peppers, depending on your preference. Pork Binagoongan is a delicious and comforting meal that pairs perfectly with steamed rice.

Ginataang Kalabasa at Sitaw (Squash and String Beans in Coconut Milk)

Ingredients:

- 2 cups kalabasa (squash), peeled and cubed
- 2 cups sitaw (string beans), cut into 2-inch pieces
- 1 tablespoon cooking oil
- 2 cloves garlic, minced
- 1 onion, chopped
- 2 cups coconut milk
- 1 cup water or vegetable broth
- 2 pieces dried bay leaves
- Salt and pepper to taste
- Optional: shrimp or pork, peeled and deveined (if adding meat)

Instructions:

1. Heat the cooking oil in a large skillet or pot over medium heat.
2. Add the minced garlic and chopped onion to the skillet. Sauté until the onion becomes translucent and aromatic.
3. If you're adding meat, add it to the skillet and cook until it's lightly browned.
4. Once the meat is browned (if using), add the cubed kalabasa (squash) and sitaw (string beans) to the skillet. Stir to combine with the onions and garlic.
5. Pour in the coconut milk and water or vegetable broth. Add the dried bay leaves.
6. Bring the mixture to a simmer, then reduce the heat to low. Cover and let it cook for about 15-20 minutes, or until the squash and string beans are tender.
7. Once the vegetables are tender, season the dish with salt and pepper to taste. Adjust the seasoning according to your preference.
8. Remove the skillet from the heat and transfer the Ginataang Kalabasa at Sitaw to a serving dish.
9. Serve the dish hot with steamed rice on the side.
10. Enjoy the creamy and flavorful goodness of this Filipino favorite!

Ginataang Kalabasa at Sitaw is a comforting and nutritious dish that's perfect for vegetarians or as a side dish for meat dishes. Feel free to customize the recipe by adding your favorite vegetables or protein.

Beef Kare-Kare (Beef Stew in Peanut Sauce)

Ingredients:

- 2 lbs (about 900g) beef stew meat, cut into chunks
- 2 tablespoons cooking oil
- 1 onion, chopped
- 4 cloves garlic, minced
- 2 tomatoes, chopped
- 1 eggplant, sliced
- 1 bunch Chinese long beans (sitaw), cut into 2-inch pieces
- 1/2 cup peanut butter
- 4 cups beef broth
- 2 tablespoons annatto seeds (achuete)
- Salt and pepper to taste
- Shrimp paste (bagoong) for serving (optional)

Instructions:

1. Heat the cooking oil in a large pot over medium heat. Add the chopped onion and minced garlic, and sauté until fragrant.
2. Add the beef stew meat to the pot and cook until browned on all sides, about 5-7 minutes.
3. Stir in the chopped tomatoes and cook until they start to soften.
4. Add the beef broth to the pot and bring to a simmer. Cover and cook for about 1 to 1.5 hours, or until the beef is tender.
5. While the beef is cooking, prepare the annatto water. In a small saucepan, combine the annatto seeds with 1/4 cup of water. Bring to a boil, then simmer for a few minutes. Strain the annatto seeds, reserving the water.
6. Once the beef is tender, add the sliced eggplant and Chinese long beans to the pot. Simmer for another 5-7 minutes, or until the vegetables are cooked through.
7. Stir in the peanut butter and annatto water, mixing until well combined. Cook for an additional 5 minutes, stirring occasionally.
8. Season the Beef Kare-Kare with salt and pepper to taste.
9. Remove the pot from the heat and transfer the Beef Kare-Kare to a serving dish.
10. Serve the Beef Kare-Kare hot, accompanied by shrimp paste (bagoong) on the side for dipping, if desired.

11. Enjoy this flavorful and hearty Filipino stew with steamed rice!

Beef Kare-Kare is often served at special occasions and gatherings, and it's best enjoyed with a side of shrimp paste for added flavor. Adjust the ingredients and seasonings according to your taste preferences.

Ginataang Hipon (Shrimp in Coconut Milk)

Ingredients:

- 1 lb (about 450g) shrimp, peeled and deveined
- 2 tablespoons cooking oil
- 1 onion, chopped
- 3 cloves garlic, minced
- 1 thumb-sized piece of ginger, sliced into thin strips
- 2 cups coconut milk
- 1 cup water or shrimp broth
- 2 cups spinach leaves or kangkong (water spinach), washed and trimmed
- 1 cup squash (kalabasa), peeled and cubed
- 1 cup string beans (sitaw), cut into 2-inch pieces
- 2 pieces green chili peppers (siling haba), sliced (optional, for added heat)
- 2 tablespoons fish sauce (patis), or to taste
- Salt and pepper to taste
- Optional garnish: chopped green onions or cilantro

Instructions:

1. Heat the cooking oil in a large pot or skillet over medium heat.
2. Add the chopped onion, minced garlic, and sliced ginger to the pot. Sauté until fragrant and the onion becomes translucent.
3. Add the cubed squash (kalabasa) to the pot and cook for a few minutes until slightly softened.
4. Pour in the coconut milk and water (or shrimp broth) into the pot. Bring the mixture to a gentle simmer.
5. Once the mixture is simmering, add the string beans (sitaw) and green chili peppers (if using). Cook for about 5 minutes, or until the vegetables are tender.
6. Add the shrimp to the pot and cook for 2-3 minutes, or until they turn pink and opaque.
7. Stir in the spinach leaves or kangkong and cook for another minute until wilted.
8. Season the Ginataang Hipon with fish sauce (patis), salt, and pepper to taste. Adjust the seasoning according to your preference.
9. Remove the pot from the heat and transfer the Ginataang Hipon to a serving dish.
10. Garnish with chopped green onions or cilantro, if desired.

11. Serve the Ginataang Hipon hot with steamed rice on the side.
12. Enjoy the creamy and flavorful goodness of this Filipino shrimp dish!

Ginataang Hipon is a comforting and satisfying meal that's perfect for lunch or dinner.

Feel free to adjust the ingredients and seasonings according to your taste preferences.

Chicken Afritada (Chicken Stewed in Tomato Sauce)

Ingredients:

- 2 lbs (about 900g) chicken pieces (legs, thighs, or breast), cut into serving portions
- 2 tablespoons cooking oil
- 1 onion, chopped
- 4 cloves garlic, minced
- 2 tomatoes, chopped
- 1 bell pepper (red or green), sliced
- 1 carrot, sliced
- 1 potato, peeled and cubed
- 1 cup green peas (fresh or frozen)
- 1 cup tomato sauce
- 1 cup chicken broth or water
- 2 bay leaves
- Salt and pepper to taste
- Optional garnish: chopped green onions or cilantro

Instructions:

1. Heat the cooking oil in a large pot or Dutch oven over medium heat.
2. Add the chopped onion and minced garlic to the pot. Sauté until fragrant and the onion becomes translucent.
3. Add the chicken pieces to the pot and cook until browned on all sides, about 5-7 minutes.
4. Stir in the chopped tomatoes and cook until they start to soften.
5. Add the sliced bell pepper, carrot, and potato to the pot. Stir to combine with the chicken and tomatoes.
6. Pour in the tomato sauce and chicken broth (or water). Add the bay leaves. Bring the mixture to a simmer.
7. Once the mixture is simmering, cover the pot and let it cook for about 30-40 minutes, or until the chicken is tender and cooked through.
8. Add the green peas to the pot during the last 5 minutes of cooking.
9. Season the Chicken Afritada with salt and pepper to taste.
10. Remove the pot from the heat and transfer the Chicken Afritada to a serving dish.

11. Garnish with chopped green onions or cilantro, if desired.
12. Serve the Chicken Afritada hot with steamed rice on the side.
13. Enjoy the delicious flavors of this Filipino favorite!

Chicken Afritada is a comforting and hearty dish that's perfect for family dinners and gatherings. Feel free to customize the recipe by adding other vegetables like green beans or olives. Adjust the seasoning according to your taste preferences.

Sisig (Sizzling Pork or Chicken)

Ingredients:

- 1 lb (about 450g) pork belly, chopped into small pieces (you can also use chicken thighs or a combination of both)
- 1 onion, finely chopped
- 3 cloves garlic, minced
- 2-3 green chili peppers (siling labuyo), chopped (adjust to taste)
- 2 tablespoons soy sauce
- 2 tablespoons calamansi juice or lemon juice
- 1 tablespoon mayonnaise
- Salt and pepper to taste
- Cooking oil for frying
- Optional garnish: chopped green onions, sliced red chili peppers, calamansi or lemon wedges

Instructions:

1. Heat some cooking oil in a skillet or frying pan over medium-high heat.
2. Add the chopped pork belly (or chicken) to the skillet and cook until browned and crispy, stirring occasionally. This may take about 8-10 minutes.
3. Once the meat is crispy, remove it from the skillet and set it aside on a plate lined with paper towels to drain excess oil.
4. In the same skillet, sauté the minced garlic and chopped onion until fragrant and translucent.
5. Add the chopped green chili peppers and continue to sauté for another minute.
6. Return the crispy pork (or chicken) to the skillet. Stir in the soy sauce and calamansi juice (or lemon juice). Mix well to combine.
7. Add the mayonnaise to the skillet and stir until it coats the meat evenly. Cook for another 2-3 minutes.
8. Season the sisig with salt and pepper to taste. Adjust the seasoning according to your preference.
9. Transfer the sisig to a sizzling hot plate if available, or serve it directly from the skillet.
10. Garnish the sisig with chopped green onions, sliced red chili peppers, and calamansi or lemon wedges.

11. Serve the sisig hot as an appetizer or main dish, along with steamed rice.
12. Enjoy the sizzling and flavorful goodness of this Filipino favorite!

Sisig is often enjoyed as a pulutan (appetizer) with drinks, but it's also delicious as a main dish served with rice. Feel free to customize the recipe by adding ingredients like chopped liver, onions, or even egg for extra richness and flavor. Adjust the amount of chili peppers according to your preferred level of spiciness.

Pinakbet (Mixed Vegetables in Shrimp Paste)

Ingredients:

- 1 small bitter melon (ampalaya), seeded and sliced
- 1 small eggplant, sliced
- 1 medium-sized squash (kalabasa), peeled and cubed
- 1 cup string beans (sitaw), cut into 2-inch pieces
- 1 medium-sized tomato, sliced
- 1 onion, sliced
- 2 cloves garlic, minced
- 2 tablespoons cooking oil
- 2 tablespoons shrimp paste (bagoong)
- 1 cup water or vegetable broth
- Salt and pepper to taste

Instructions:

1. Heat the cooking oil in a large pan or wok over medium heat.
2. Add the minced garlic and sliced onion to the pan. Sauté until fragrant and the onion becomes translucent.
3. Stir in the sliced tomato and cook until softened.
4. Add the bitter melon (ampalaya), eggplant, squash (kalabasa), and string beans (sitaw) to the pan. Stir-fry the vegetables for about 3-5 minutes.
5. Mix in the shrimp paste (bagoong) and continue to cook for another 2 minutes, stirring occasionally to evenly distribute the flavors.
6. Pour in the water or vegetable broth and bring the mixture to a simmer.
7. Cover the pan and let the vegetables cook for about 10-15 minutes, or until they are tender but still slightly crisp.
8. Season the Pinakbet with salt and pepper to taste. Adjust the seasoning according to your preference.
9. Once the vegetables are cooked and the flavors have melded together, remove the pan from the heat.
10. Transfer the Pinakbet to a serving dish and serve hot with steamed rice.
11. Enjoy the savory and flavorful taste of this traditional Filipino dish!

Pinakbet is a versatile dish, and you can adjust the ingredients according to your preference or what's available. Some variations include adding shrimp, pork, or fish sauce (patis) for extra flavor. Feel free to experiment and make it your own!

Laing (Taro Leaves in Coconut Milk)

Ingredients:

- 2 cups dried taro leaves (dahon ng gabi), stems removed
- 1 cup coconut milk
- 1 cup coconut cream (kakang gata)
- 1 onion, chopped
- 3 cloves garlic, minced
- 2 tablespoons shrimp paste (bagoong alamang)
- 2 cups water or vegetable broth
- 2-3 pieces dried chili peppers (siling labuyo), chopped (adjust to taste)
- 1 tablespoon cooking oil
- Salt and pepper to taste

Instructions:

1. Heat the cooking oil in a large pan or pot over medium heat.
2. Sauté the minced garlic and chopped onion until fragrant and translucent.
3. Add the shrimp paste (bagoong alamang) to the pan and cook for another minute, stirring constantly.
4. Pour in the coconut milk and water (or vegetable broth) into the pan. Stir to combine.
5. Add the dried taro leaves to the pan. Make sure they are submerged in the liquid. If needed, you can break them into smaller pieces.
6. Cover the pan and let the mixture simmer for about 20-25 minutes, stirring occasionally, or until the taro leaves are tender and cooked through.
7. Once the taro leaves are cooked, add the coconut cream (kakang gata) to the pan. Stir well to combine.
8. Add the chopped dried chili peppers to the pan for some heat, if desired. Stir to distribute evenly.
9. Season the Laing with salt and pepper to taste. Adjust the seasoning according to your preference.
10. Let the Laing simmer uncovered for another 5-10 minutes, or until the sauce thickens and reduces slightly.
11. Once the Laing reaches your desired consistency, remove the pan from the heat.
12. Transfer the Laing to a serving dish and serve hot with steamed rice.
13. Enjoy the creamy and flavorful goodness of this traditional Filipino dish!

Laing is best enjoyed hot and pairs perfectly with steamed rice. Feel free to adjust the amount of chili peppers according to your preferred level of spiciness. You can also add other ingredients like pork or shrimp for variation.

Pork Adobo Flakes

Ingredients:

- 1 lb (about 450g) pork belly or pork shoulder, cooked and shredded (you can use leftover pork adobo or cook the pork specifically for this dish)
- 2 tablespoons cooking oil
- 3 cloves garlic, minced
- 1 onion, finely chopped
- 1/4 cup soy sauce
- 1/4 cup vinegar
- 1 bay leaf
- 1/2 teaspoon whole peppercorns
- Salt and pepper to taste
- Steamed rice, for serving

Instructions:

1. If you're not using leftover pork adobo, you can cook the pork specifically for this dish by following these steps:
    - In a pot, combine the pork pieces, soy sauce, vinegar, minced garlic, chopped onion, bay leaf, and whole peppercorns.
    - Bring the mixture to a boil, then lower the heat to a simmer. Cook until the pork is tender and the flavors have melded together, about 45 minutes to 1 hour.
    - Once the pork is cooked, remove it from the pot and shred it using two forks or your hands. Reserve the cooking liquid for later use.
2. Heat the cooking oil in a large skillet over medium heat.
3. Add the shredded pork to the skillet and cook until it starts to brown and crisp up, stirring occasionally. This may take about 10-15 minutes.
4. If the pork starts to stick to the skillet, you can add a bit of the reserved cooking liquid from the pork adobo to help loosen it up.
5. Continue cooking until the pork is crispy and golden brown. Adjust the heat as needed to prevent burning.
6. Once the pork is crispy, remove the skillet from the heat and season the pork adobo flakes with salt and pepper to taste.
7. Transfer the pork adobo flakes to a serving dish and serve hot with steamed rice.

8. Enjoy the delicious crispy goodness of Pork Adobo Flakes as a topping for rice or as a filling for sandwiches!

Pork Adobo Flakes are versatile and can be enjoyed in various ways. You can also serve them as a crunchy topping for salads or wraps. Adjust the seasoning according to your taste preferences, and feel free to customize the recipe with additional spices or ingredients.

Ginisang Upo (Sauteed Bottle Gourd)

Ingredients:

- 1 medium-sized bottle gourd (upo), peeled and sliced into thin strips
- 2 tablespoons cooking oil
- 1 onion, finely chopped
- 3 cloves garlic, minced
- 1 medium-sized tomato, diced
- 1/4 lb (about 115g) pork belly or shrimp, diced (optional)
- 1 cup shrimp broth or water
- Fish sauce (patis) or salt, to taste
- Ground black pepper, to taste
- Optional garnish: chopped green onions or cilantro

Instructions:

1. Heat the cooking oil in a large skillet or pan over medium heat.
2. Add the diced pork belly or shrimp to the skillet and cook until browned and slightly crispy. If omitting meat, proceed to step 3.
3. Add the minced garlic and chopped onion to the skillet. Sauté until fragrant and the onion becomes translucent.
4. Stir in the diced tomato and cook until softened.
5. Add the sliced bottle gourd (upo) to the skillet. Stir-fry for a few minutes until the bottle gourd starts to soften.
6. Pour in the shrimp broth or water into the skillet. Cover and let it simmer for about 5-7 minutes, or until the bottle gourd is tender but still slightly crisp.
7. Season the Ginisang Upo with fish sauce (patis) or salt, and ground black pepper to taste. Adjust the seasoning according to your preference.
8. Continue to cook for another minute or two to allow the flavors to meld together.
9. Once the bottle gourd is cooked to your liking and the flavors are well combined, remove the skillet from the heat.
10. Transfer the Ginisang Upo to a serving dish and garnish with chopped green onions or cilantro, if desired.
11. Serve hot with steamed rice.
12. Enjoy the simple and delicious flavors of this Filipino dish!

Ginisang Upo is a versatile dish that can be enjoyed on its own or served as a side dish to complement other Filipino favorites. Feel free to customize the recipe by adding other vegetables or protein according to your preference. Adjust the seasoning and spiciness level to suit your taste.

Bangus (Milkfish) Belly Paksiw

Ingredients:

- 4 pieces bangus (milkfish) belly, cleaned and sliced into serving pieces
- 1 cup vinegar
- 1 cup water
- 1/2 cup soy sauce
- 1 onion, sliced
- 3 cloves garlic, minced
- 2-3 pieces dried bay leaves
- 1 teaspoon whole peppercorns
- 1 tablespoon brown sugar
- Salt, to taste
- Cooking oil, for sautéing
- Optional: sliced red chili peppers for added heat
- Steamed rice, for serving

Instructions:

1. In a large pot or pan, heat a small amount of cooking oil over medium heat.
2. Sauté the minced garlic and sliced onion until fragrant and translucent.
3. Add the sliced bangus belly pieces to the pot, arranging them in a single layer.
4. Pour in the vinegar and water. Add the soy sauce, dried bay leaves, whole peppercorns, and brown sugar. Stir gently to combine.
5. If using red chili peppers for added heat, add them to the pot.
6. Bring the mixture to a boil, then lower the heat to a simmer. Cover and let it cook for about 10-15 minutes, or until the fish is cooked through and tender.
7. Once the fish is cooked, taste the sauce and adjust the seasoning with salt if needed.
8. Remove the pot from the heat and transfer the Bangus Belly Paksiw to a serving dish.
9. Serve hot with steamed rice.
10. Enjoy the tangy and savory flavors of this Filipino dish!

Bangus Belly Paksiw is best enjoyed with steamed rice and some sliced tomatoes or cucumber on the side. The vinegar-based sauce helps preserve the fish and gives it a deliciously tangy flavor. Feel free to adjust the sweetness and acidity of the sauce according to your taste preferences.

Ginataang Langka (Young Jackfruit in Coconut Milk)

Ingredients:

- 1 medium-sized young jackfruit (langka), peeled and sliced into bite-sized pieces
- 2 cups coconut milk
- 1 onion, chopped
- 3 cloves garlic, minced
- 1 thumb-sized piece of ginger, sliced into thin strips
- 2-3 pieces dried bay leaves
- 1 cup shrimp or pork, peeled and deveined (optional)
- 2 tablespoons fish sauce (patis), or to taste
- Salt and pepper to taste
- Cooking oil for sautéing
- Optional: sliced red chili peppers for added heat
- Steamed rice, for serving

Instructions:

1. Heat a small amount of cooking oil in a large pot or skillet over medium heat.
2. Sauté the minced garlic, chopped onion, and sliced ginger until fragrant and translucent.
3. If using shrimp or pork, add it to the pot and cook until lightly browned.
4. Add the sliced young jackfruit (langka) to the pot and stir to combine with the other ingredients.
5. Pour in the coconut milk and add the dried bay leaves to the pot. Stir gently to combine.
6. Bring the mixture to a simmer, then lower the heat to medium-low. Cover and let it cook for about 15-20 minutes, or until the young jackfruit is tender.
7. Once the young jackfruit is tender, season the Ginataang Langka with fish sauce (patis), salt, and pepper to taste. Adjust the seasoning according to your preference.
8. If using red chili peppers for added heat, add them to the pot and stir to incorporate.
9. Let the Ginataang Langka simmer uncovered for another 5 minutes to allow the flavors to meld together.

10. Remove the pot from the heat and transfer the Ginataang Langka to a serving dish.
11. Serve hot with steamed rice.
12. Enjoy the creamy and flavorful goodness of this Filipino dish!

Ginataang Langka is a comforting and satisfying dish that's perfect for vegetarians or as a side dish for meat dishes. Feel free to customize the recipe by adding other vegetables or protein according to your preference. Adjust the seasoning and spiciness level to suit your taste.

Ginisang Sayote (Sauteed Chayote)

Ingredients:

- 2 chayote squash, peeled, seeded, and sliced thinly
- 2 tablespoons cooking oil
- 1 onion, sliced
- 3 cloves garlic, minced
- 2 tomatoes, diced
- 1/4 lb (about 115g) pork belly or shrimp, diced (optional)
- 1 cup water or vegetable broth
- Fish sauce (patis) or salt, to taste
- Ground black pepper, to taste
- Optional: sliced red chili peppers for added heat
- Steamed rice, for serving

Instructions:

1. Heat the cooking oil in a large skillet or pan over medium heat.
2. Add the diced pork belly or shrimp to the skillet and cook until browned. If you're not using meat, you can skip this step.
3. Once the meat is cooked, add the minced garlic and sliced onion to the skillet. Sauté until the onion becomes translucent and the garlic is fragrant.
4. Add the diced tomatoes to the skillet and cook until they start to soften.
5. Incorporate the sliced chayote squash into the skillet. Stir well to combine with the other ingredients.
6. Pour in the water or vegetable broth and bring the mixture to a simmer. Cover and let it cook for about 5-7 minutes, or until the chayote is tender.
7. Season the Ginisang Sayote with fish sauce (patis) or salt and ground black pepper to taste. Adjust the seasoning according to your preference.
8. If you prefer some heat, you can add sliced red chili peppers to the skillet and stir to incorporate.
9. Let the dish simmer for another minute or two to allow the flavors to meld together.
10. Once the chayote is cooked to your liking and the flavors have infused, remove the skillet from the heat.
11. Transfer the Ginisang Sayote to a serving dish.

12. Serve hot with steamed rice.
13. Enjoy the delightful flavors and comforting simplicity of this Filipino dish!

Ginisang Sayote is perfect as a standalone dish or as a side to complement other Filipino meals. Feel free to adjust the ingredients and seasoning according to your taste preferences.

Bicol Express (Spicy Pork in Coconut Milk)

Ingredients:

- 1 lb (about 450g) pork belly, thinly sliced
- 2 cups coconut milk
- 4-5 pieces Thai chili peppers (siling labuyo), chopped (adjust to taste)
- 4 cloves garlic, minced
- 1 onion, chopped
- 2 tablespoons shrimp paste (bagoong alamang)
- 1 tablespoon cooking oil
- Salt and pepper to taste
- Optional: sliced green chili peppers for garnish
- Steamed rice, for serving

Instructions:

1. Heat the cooking oil in a large skillet or pan over medium heat.
2. Add the minced garlic and chopped onion to the skillet. Sauté until fragrant and the onion becomes translucent.
3. Add the thinly sliced pork belly to the skillet. Cook until the pork is browned and slightly crispy.
4. Stir in the chopped Thai chili peppers and shrimp paste (bagoong alamang). Cook for another minute to allow the flavors to meld together.
5. Pour in the coconut milk into the skillet. Stir well to combine with the other ingredients.
6. Bring the mixture to a simmer, then lower the heat to medium-low. Let it cook for about 20-25 minutes, or until the pork is tender and the sauce has thickened.
7. Season the Bicol Express with salt and pepper to taste. Adjust the seasoning according to your preference.
8. If desired, garnish with sliced green chili peppers for an extra kick of heat.
9. Once the pork is cooked and the sauce has thickened to your liking, remove the skillet from the heat.
10. Transfer the Bicol Express to a serving dish.
11. Serve hot with steamed rice.
12. Enjoy the spicy and creamy goodness of this classic Filipino dish!

Bicol Express is perfect for spice lovers and pairs wonderfully with steamed rice to balance out the heat. Adjust the amount of chili peppers according to your preferred level of spiciness. Feel free to customize the recipe by adding other ingredients like shrimp or vegetables.

Beef Sinigang (Beef Sour Soup)

Ingredients:

- 1 lb (about 450g) beef shank, brisket, or ribs, cut into serving pieces
- 1 onion, quartered
- 2 tomatoes, quartered
- 1 radish (labanos), peeled and sliced
- 1 eggplant, sliced
- 1 bunch kangkong (water spinach) or spinach, leaves separated from stems
- 8-10 pieces string beans (sitaw), cut into 2-inch lengths
- 2-3 pieces green chili peppers (siling haba)
- 1 packet (about 40g) tamarind soup base mix (sinigang mix)
- 2 liters water
- Fish sauce (patis) or salt, to taste
- Ground black pepper, to taste
- Steamed rice, for serving

Instructions:

1. In a large pot, bring the water to a boil over medium heat.
2. Add the beef pieces to the pot. Let it boil for about 10 minutes, skimming off any scum that rises to the surface.
3. Once the beef is partially cooked, add the quartered onion and tomatoes to the pot. Let it simmer for another 10 minutes.
4. Stir in the tamarind soup base mix (sinigang mix) into the pot. Mix well to dissolve the mix into the broth.
5. Add the sliced radish (labanos) and string beans (sitaw) to the pot. Let it simmer for about 10 minutes, or until the vegetables are tender.
6. Add the sliced eggplant to the pot and let it simmer for another 5 minutes.
7. Season the Beef Sinigang with fish sauce (patis) or salt and ground black pepper to taste. Adjust the seasoning according to your preference.
8. Add the kangkong leaves (or spinach) and green chili peppers (siling haba) to the pot. Let it simmer for a couple of minutes until the leaves are wilted.
9. Once the beef is tender and the vegetables are cooked, remove the pot from the heat.
10. Transfer the Beef Sinigang to a serving bowl.

11. Serve hot with steamed rice.
12. Enjoy the comforting and tangy flavors of this classic Filipino soup!

Beef Sinigang is perfect for warming up on chilly days and is best enjoyed with steamed rice and a side of fish sauce with calamansi or lemon juice. Adjust the sourness level by adding more tamarind soup base mix according to your preference.

Chicken Tinola sa Papaya (Chicken Soup with Papaya)

Ingredients:

- 1 whole chicken, cut into serving pieces
- 1 small green papaya, peeled, seeded, and sliced into wedges
- 1 thumb-sized ginger, sliced thinly
- 3 cloves garlic, minced
- 1 onion, chopped
- 2 tablespoons cooking oil
- 1 bunch spinach or chili leaves, washed and trimmed
- 1-2 pieces green chili peppers (siling haba), optional
- Fish sauce (patis) or salt, to taste
- Ground black pepper, to taste
- 2 liters water
- Steamed rice, for serving

Instructions:

1. Heat the cooking oil in a large pot over medium heat.
2. Add the minced garlic and sliced ginger to the pot. Sauté until fragrant.
3. Add the chopped onion to the pot. Sauté until the onion becomes translucent.
4. Add the chicken pieces to the pot. Cook until they are lightly browned.
5. Pour in the water into the pot. Bring it to a boil, then lower the heat to a simmer. Let it cook for about 20-25 minutes, or until the chicken is tender.
6. Once the chicken is tender, add the sliced green papaya to the pot. Let it simmer for about 5-7 minutes, or until the papaya is tender but still slightly crisp.
7. Season the Chicken Tinola with fish sauce (patis) or salt and ground black pepper to taste. Adjust the seasoning according to your preference.
8. Add the spinach or chili leaves to the pot. Let them wilt in the broth for a minute or two.
9. If using green chili peppers, add them to the pot for an extra kick of heat.
10. Once the vegetables are cooked and the flavors have melded together, remove the pot from the heat.
11. Transfer the Chicken Tinola sa Papaya to a serving bowl.
12. Serve hot with steamed rice.
13. Enjoy the comforting and nourishing flavors of this classic Filipino soup!

Chicken Tinola sa Papaya is perfect for warming up on chilly days and is best enjoyed with steamed rice and a side of fish sauce with calamansi or lemon juice. Feel free to adjust the ingredients and seasoning according to your taste preferences.

Pininyahang Manok (Chicken with Pineapple)

Ingredients:

- 1 whole chicken, cut into serving pieces
- 1 can (about 400g) pineapple chunks, drained (reserve the juice)
- 1 onion, sliced
- 3 cloves garlic, minced
- 1 thumb-sized ginger, sliced thinly
- 2 tablespoons cooking oil
- 1 cup coconut milk
- 1 red bell pepper, sliced
- 1 green bell pepper, sliced
- 2-3 pieces green chili peppers (siling haba), optional
- Fish sauce (patis) or salt, to taste
- Ground black pepper, to taste
- Steamed rice, for serving

Instructions:

1. Heat the cooking oil in a large skillet or pan over medium heat.
2. Add the minced garlic and sliced ginger to the skillet. Sauté until fragrant.
3. Add the sliced onion to the skillet. Sauté until the onion becomes translucent.
4. Add the chicken pieces to the skillet. Cook until they are lightly browned on all sides.
5. Pour in the coconut milk and reserved pineapple juice into the skillet. Bring it to a simmer.
6. Let the chicken simmer in the coconut milk and pineapple juice mixture for about 15-20 minutes, or until the chicken is almost cooked through.
7. Add the drained pineapple chunks to the skillet. Stir well to combine with the chicken and sauce.
8. Add the sliced red and green bell peppers to the skillet. Stir to incorporate.
9. If using green chili peppers for added heat, add them to the skillet as well.
10. Season the Pininyahang Manok with fish sauce (patis) or salt and ground black pepper to taste. Adjust the seasoning according to your preference.
11. Let the dish simmer for another 5-10 minutes, or until the chicken is fully cooked and the sauce has thickened slightly.

12. Once the chicken is cooked through and the flavors have melded together, remove the skillet from the heat.
13. Transfer the Pininyahang Manok to a serving dish.
14. Serve hot with steamed rice.
15. Enjoy the deliciously sweet and savory flavors of this classic Filipino dish!

Pininyahang Manok is perfect for family dinners and gatherings, and it pairs wonderfully with steamed rice. Feel free to customize the recipe by adding other vegetables like carrots or potatoes, or adjusting the amount of pineapple according to your taste preferences.

Dinuguan (Pork Blood Stew)

Ingredients:

- 1 lb (about 450g) pork belly or pork shoulder, diced
- 1/2 lb (about 225g) pork offal (such as liver, heart, or intestines), diced (optional)
- 1 cup pork blood (fresh or frozen), mixed with 1 cup water
- 1 onion, chopped
- 3 cloves garlic, minced
- 2-3 pieces green chili peppers (siling haba), sliced (optional)
- 2 tablespoons cooking oil
- 2 cups pork broth or water
- 2 tablespoons vinegar
- 3-4 pieces dried bay leaves
- Salt and pepper to taste
- Steamed rice, for serving

Instructions:

1. Heat the cooking oil in a large pot over medium heat.
2. Add the minced garlic and chopped onion to the pot. Sauté until fragrant and the onion becomes translucent.
3. Add the diced pork meat and offal to the pot. Cook until lightly browned.
4. Pour in the pork broth or water into the pot. Add the dried bay leaves and sliced green chili peppers if using. Bring it to a boil, then lower the heat to a simmer.
5. Let the mixture simmer for about 30-40 minutes, or until the pork meat and offal are tender.
6. Once the meat is tender, pour in the mixed pork blood and water into the pot. Stir well to combine.
7. Add the vinegar to the pot. Stir to incorporate.
8. Let the mixture simmer for another 10-15 minutes, stirring occasionally, until the sauce thickens and the flavors meld together.
9. Season the Dinuguan with salt and pepper to taste. Adjust the seasoning according to your preference.
10. Once the sauce has thickened to your liking and the flavors have melded together, remove the pot from the heat.
11. Transfer the Dinuguan to a serving dish.
12. Serve hot with steamed rice.

13. Enjoy the rich and savory flavors of this classic Filipino dish!

Dinuguan is best enjoyed fresh and pairs well with steamed rice or puto (steamed rice cakes). Feel free to adjust the amount of chili peppers and vinegar according to your taste preferences.

Ginisang Ampalaya (Sauteed Bitter Melon)

Ingredients:

- 2 medium-sized bitter melons (ampalaya), sliced and seeds removed
- 1 onion, sliced
- 3 cloves garlic, minced
- 2 medium-sized tomatoes, chopped
- 2 eggs, beaten
- 1/4 lb (about 115g) pork belly or shrimp, diced (optional)
- 2 tablespoons cooking oil
- Fish sauce (patis) or salt, to taste
- Ground black pepper, to taste
- Steamed rice, for serving

Instructions:

1. Heat the cooking oil in a large skillet or pan over medium heat.
2. If using pork belly or shrimp, add them to the skillet and cook until browned. If omitting meat, proceed to step 3.
3. Add the minced garlic to the skillet. Sauté until fragrant.
4. Add the sliced onion to the skillet. Sauté until the onion becomes translucent.
5. Add the chopped tomatoes to the skillet. Cook until they start to soften.
6. Add the sliced bitter melon (ampalaya) to the skillet. Stir well to combine with the other ingredients.
7. Let the bitter melon cook for about 5-7 minutes, or until slightly tender.
8. Pour the beaten eggs over the bitter melon mixture. Allow the eggs to set slightly before stirring to scramble them with the vegetables.
9. Season the Ginisang Ampalaya with fish sauce (patis) or salt and ground black pepper to taste. Adjust the seasoning according to your preference.
10. Continue to cook for another 2-3 minutes, or until the bitter melon is cooked to your liking and the flavors have melded together.
11. Once the bitter melon is cooked and the flavors have melded together, remove the skillet from the heat.
12. Transfer the Ginisang Ampalaya to a serving dish.
13. Serve hot with steamed rice.
14. Enjoy the delicious and nutritious flavors of this Filipino dish!

Ginisang Ampalaya is perfect for those looking for a nutritious and flavorful meal. The bitterness of the melon is balanced out by the savory ingredients, making it a satisfying dish. Feel free to adjust the ingredients and seasoning according to your taste preferences.

Inihaw na Liempo (Grilled Pork Belly)

Ingredients:

- 1 lb (about 450g) pork belly, sliced into thin strips
- 1/4 cup soy sauce
- 1/4 cup calamansi juice or lemon juice
- 3 cloves garlic, minced
- 1 teaspoon ground black pepper
- 2 tablespoons brown sugar
- Cooking oil, for brushing
- Bamboo skewers, soaked in water for at least 30 minutes
- Steamed rice and dipping sauce (suka't bawang or soy sauce with calamansi) for serving

Instructions:

1. In a bowl, combine the soy sauce, calamansi juice (or lemon juice), minced garlic, ground black pepper, and brown sugar. Mix well to dissolve the sugar and create the marinade.
2. Place the sliced pork belly in a shallow dish or resealable plastic bag. Pour the marinade over the pork belly, making sure it is evenly coated. Marinate the pork belly in the refrigerator for at least 1 hour, or preferably overnight for maximum flavor.
3. Preheat your grill to medium-high heat.
4. Thread the marinated pork belly slices onto the soaked bamboo skewers, dividing them evenly.
5. Brush the grill grates with cooking oil to prevent the pork from sticking. Place the skewers of pork belly on the grill.
6. Grill the pork belly for about 4-5 minutes on each side, or until nicely charred and cooked through. Baste the pork belly with any remaining marinade while grilling for added flavor.
7. Once the pork belly is cooked through and charred to your liking, remove the skewers from the grill.
8. Transfer the Inihaw na Liempo to a serving platter.
9. Serve hot with steamed rice and your choice of dipping sauce.
10. Enjoy the smoky, savory goodness of this classic Filipino dish!

Inihaw na Liempo is perfect for gatherings, parties, or as a delicious meal any day of the week. Adjust the marinade ingredients according to your taste preferences, and feel free to add additional seasonings or spices for extra flavor.

Binakol (Chicken Soup with Coconut Water)

Ingredients:

- 1 whole chicken, cut into serving pieces
- 4 cups coconut water
- 1 cup coconut milk
- 1 onion, sliced
- 3 cloves garlic, minced
- 1 thumb-sized ginger, sliced thinly
- 2 medium-sized tomatoes, quartered
- 1 medium-sized green papaya, peeled, seeded, and sliced
- 2 pieces green chili peppers (siling haba), optional
- Fish sauce (patis) or salt, to taste
- Ground black pepper, to taste
- 1 bunch spinach or chili leaves, washed and trimmed
- Steamed rice, for serving

Instructions:

1. In a large pot, combine the coconut water, coconut milk, sliced onion, minced garlic, sliced ginger, and quartered tomatoes.
2. Bring the mixture to a boil over medium heat.
3. Once boiling, add the chicken pieces to the pot. Let it simmer for about 20-25 minutes, or until the chicken is partially cooked.
4. Add the sliced green papaya to the pot. Continue to simmer for another 10-15 minutes, or until the papaya is tender.
5. Season the Binakol with fish sauce (patis) or salt and ground black pepper to taste. Adjust the seasoning according to your preference.
6. If using green chili peppers for added heat, add them to the pot.
7. Add the spinach or chili leaves to the pot. Let them wilt in the broth for a minute or two.
8. Once the chicken is fully cooked, the papaya is tender, and the flavors have melded together, remove the pot from the heat.
9. Transfer the Binakol to a serving bowl.
10. Serve hot with steamed rice.
11. Enjoy the refreshing and savory flavors of this classic Filipino soup!

Binakol is perfect for warming up on chilly days and is best enjoyed with steamed rice. The combination of coconut water and coconut milk gives the soup a unique and refreshing taste. Feel free to adjust the ingredients and seasoning according to your taste preferences.

Kilawin (Filipino Ceviche)

Ingredients:

- 1 lb (about 450g) fresh fish fillets (such as tuna, tanigue/mackerel, or tilapia), cubed
- 1 cup vinegar (cane vinegar or white vinegar)
- Juice of 3-4 calamansi or 1-2 limes
- 1 medium-sized red onion, thinly sliced
- 1 medium-sized tomato, diced
- 1 thumb-sized ginger, peeled and minced
- 2-3 pieces green chili peppers (siling labuyo or Thai bird's eye chili), sliced (optional)
- Salt and pepper to taste
- 1/4 cup coconut cream (optional)
- Fresh cilantro or kinchay (Chinese celery), chopped, for garnish
- Thinly sliced red chili peppers, for garnish (optional)
- Lettuce leaves, for serving

Instructions:

1. In a bowl, combine the vinegar and calamansi or lime juice to create the marinade.
2. Add the cubed fish fillets to the marinade, ensuring they are fully submerged. Let the fish marinate in the refrigerator for about 30 minutes to 1 hour. The acidity of the vinegar and citrus juices will "cook" the fish.
3. After marinating, drain the fish and discard the marinade. Transfer the fish to a clean bowl.
4. Add the thinly sliced red onion, diced tomato, minced ginger, and sliced green chili peppers (if using) to the bowl with the fish.
5. Season the Kilawin with salt and pepper to taste. Mix well to combine all the ingredients.
6. If desired, add coconut cream to the Kilawin for added creaminess. Mix gently to incorporate.
7. Transfer the Kilawin to a serving dish lined with lettuce leaves.
8. Garnish the Kilawin with chopped fresh cilantro or kinchay, and thinly sliced red chili peppers (if using).

9. Serve immediately as an appetizer or main dish, alongside steamed rice or as a pulutan (beer snack).
10. Enjoy the fresh and tangy flavors of this Filipino ceviche!

Kilawin is best enjoyed fresh, as the flavors are brightest when served immediately after preparation. Adjust the amount of chili peppers according to your preferred level of spiciness. You can also customize the dish by adding other ingredients such as diced cucumber or mango for additional texture and sweetness.

Ginisang Monggo (Mung Bean Soup)

Ingredients:

- 1 cup mung beans (monggo), washed and drained
- 4 cups water
- 2 tablespoons cooking oil
- 3 cloves garlic, minced
- 1 onion, chopped
- 2 medium-sized tomatoes, chopped
- 1/4 lb (about 115g) pork belly or pork shoulder, diced
- 1 cup spinach or malunggay leaves (moringa), washed and trimmed
- Fish sauce (patis) or salt, to taste
- Ground black pepper, to taste
- Optional toppings: sliced green onions, crispy fried garlic

Instructions:

1. In a pot, combine the washed mung beans and water. Bring it to a boil over medium heat.
2. Once boiling, reduce the heat to low and let the mung beans simmer for about 30-40 minutes, or until they are soft and fully cooked. Stir occasionally and add more water if needed to prevent sticking.
3. While the mung beans are cooking, heat the cooking oil in a separate pan over medium heat.
4. Add the minced garlic to the pan. Sauté until golden brown and fragrant.
5. Add the chopped onion to the pan. Sauté until the onion becomes translucent.
6. Add the diced pork belly or pork shoulder to the pan. Cook until browned and caramelized.
7. Once the pork is cooked, add the chopped tomatoes to the pan. Cook until they start to soften.
8. Transfer the sautéed garlic, onion, pork, and tomatoes to the pot with the cooked mung beans. Mix well to combine.
9. Season the Ginisang Monggo with fish sauce (patis) or salt and ground black pepper to taste. Adjust the seasoning according to your preference.
10. Let the soup simmer for another 5-10 minutes to allow the flavors to meld together.

11. Add the spinach or malunggay leaves to the pot. Let them wilt in the soup for a minute or two.
12. Once the vegetables are cooked and the flavors have melded together, remove the pot from the heat.
13. Transfer the Ginisang Monggo to serving bowls.
14. Garnish with sliced green onions and crispy fried garlic, if desired.
15. Serve hot with steamed rice.
16. Enjoy the hearty and nutritious flavors of this Filipino Mung Bean Soup!

Ginisang Monggo is perfect for warming up on chilly days and is packed with protein and fiber from the mung beans and vegetables. Feel free to customize the recipe by adding other vegetables such as squash or eggplant, or by using different types of meat or seafood.

Ginisang Labanos (Sauteed Radish)

Ingredients:

- 2 large radishes (labanos), peeled and sliced thinly
- 2 tablespoons cooking oil
- 3 cloves garlic, minced
- 1 small onion, chopped
- 1 medium-sized tomato, chopped
- Salt and pepper to taste
- Optional: sliced green onions or chopped cilantro for garnish

Instructions:

1. Heat the cooking oil in a pan over medium heat.
2. Add the minced garlic to the pan. Saute until golden brown and fragrant.
3. Add the chopped onion to the pan. Saute until the onion becomes translucent.
4. Add the chopped tomato to the pan. Cook until the tomato starts to soften.
5. Add the thinly sliced radishes to the pan. Stir well to combine with the other ingredients.
6. Saute the radishes for about 5-7 minutes, or until they are tender but still slightly crisp.
7. Season the Ginisang Labanos with salt and pepper to taste. Adjust the seasoning according to your preference.
8. Once the radishes are cooked to your liking and the flavors have melded together, remove the pan from the heat.
9. Transfer the Ginisang Labanos to a serving dish.
10. Garnish with sliced green onions or chopped cilantro, if desired.
11. Serve hot as a side dish or as a main dish with steamed rice.
12. Enjoy the simple and delicious flavors of this Filipino Sauteed Radish dish!

Ginisang Labanos is a versatile dish that can be easily customized to your taste preferences. Feel free to add other vegetables such as carrots or bell peppers for extra flavor and color. You can also add protein like sliced pork or shrimp to make it a heartier meal.

Balut (Fertilized Duck Egg)

Ingredients:

- Fertilized duck eggs (balut)
- Water
- Salt

Instructions:

1. Select fresh fertilized duck eggs from a reputable source. Balut eggs are typically about 14 to 21 days old.
2. Rinse the duck eggs thoroughly under cold water to remove any dirt or debris.
3. In a large pot, add enough water to fully submerge the duck eggs.
4. Place the duck eggs in the pot of water and bring it to a boil over medium-high heat.
5. Once the water reaches a boil, reduce the heat to medium-low and let the eggs simmer for about 15 to 20 minutes.
6. While the eggs are boiling, occasionally rotate them gently with a spoon to ensure even cooking.
7. After 15 to 20 minutes, remove the pot from the heat and carefully drain the hot water.
8. Fill a large bowl with cold water and ice cubes. Transfer the boiled duck eggs to the ice water bath to stop the cooking process and cool them down quickly.
9. Once the eggs have cooled down, carefully crack the shell open at the wider end using a spoon or knife.
10. Season the exposed contents of the egg with a pinch of salt, if desired.
11. Hold the egg with one hand and use the other hand to gently sip the flavorful broth inside the egg.
12. Continue to peel away the shell and enjoy the soft contents of the egg, including the partially formed duck embryo and yolk.
13. Balut is traditionally enjoyed with a sprinkle of salt or a dipping sauce made from vinegar, salt, and chili peppers.
14. Serve balut as a snack or appetizer, and enjoy the unique flavors and textures of this Filipino delicacy.

Remember, balut may not be to everyone's taste due to its unique texture and flavor profile, but it is considered a cultural delicacy in many Southeast Asian countries. Enjoy it as part of a culinary adventure or cultural experience!

Kinilaw na Isda (Fish Ceviche)

Ingredients:

- 1 lb (about 450g) fresh fish fillets (such as tuna, tanigue/mackerel, or tilapia), cubed
- 1 cup coconut vinegar or white vinegar
- Juice of 3-4 calamansi or 1-2 limes
- 1 thumb-sized ginger, peeled and minced
- 1 small red onion, thinly sliced
- 2-3 pieces red or green chili peppers (siling labuyo or Thai bird's eye chili), sliced
- 1 medium-sized tomato, diced
- Salt and pepper to taste
- 1/4 cup coconut cream (optional)
- Fresh cilantro or kinchay (Chinese celery), chopped, for garnish
- Thinly sliced red chili peppers, for garnish (optional)

Instructions:

1. In a bowl, combine the vinegar and calamansi or lime juice to create the marinade.
2. Add the cubed fish fillets to the marinade, ensuring they are fully submerged. Let the fish marinate in the refrigerator for about 15-30 minutes. The acidity of the vinegar and citrus juices will "cook" the fish.
3. After marinating, drain the fish and discard the marinade. Transfer the fish to a clean bowl.
4. Add the minced ginger, thinly sliced red onion, diced tomato, and sliced chili peppers to the bowl with the fish.
5. Season the Kinilaw na Isda with salt and pepper to taste. Mix well to combine all the ingredients.
6. If desired, add coconut cream to the Kinilaw na Isda for added creaminess. Mix gently to incorporate.
7. Transfer the Kinilaw na Isda to a serving dish.
8. Garnish with chopped fresh cilantro or kinchay, and thinly sliced red chili peppers (if using).
9. Serve immediately as an appetizer or main dish, alongside steamed rice or as a pulutan (beer snack).

10. Enjoy the fresh and tangy flavors of this Filipino Fish Ceviche!

Kinilaw na Isda is best enjoyed fresh, as the flavors are brightest when served immediately after preparation. Adjust the amount of chili peppers according to your preferred level of spiciness. You can also customize the dish by adding other ingredients such as diced cucumber or mango for additional texture and sweetness.

Pochero (Filipino Beef Stew)

Ingredients:

- 1 lb (about 450g) beef stew meat, cubed
- 2 tablespoons cooking oil
- 3 cloves garlic, minced
- 1 onion, chopped
- 2 tomatoes, chopped
- 2 tablespoons tomato paste
- 6 cups beef broth or water
- 2 potatoes, peeled and cubed
- 1 sweet potato (kamote), peeled and cubed
- 1 plantain (saba banana), peeled and sliced
- 1 small cabbage, quartered
- 1 bunch bok choy or pechay, ends trimmed
- 2-3 pieces chorizo de Bilbao or Spanish chorizo, sliced
- Salt and pepper to taste
- Fish sauce (patis) or soy sauce, to taste
- Optional garnish: chopped green onions or cilantro

Instructions:

1. Heat the cooking oil in a large pot over medium heat.
2. Add the minced garlic to the pot. Sauté until golden brown and fragrant.
3. Add the chopped onion to the pot. Sauté until the onion becomes translucent.
4. Add the cubed beef stew meat to the pot. Cook until browned on all sides.
5. Stir in the chopped tomatoes and tomato paste. Cook for a few minutes until the tomatoes start to soften.
6. Pour in the beef broth or water into the pot. Bring it to a boil, then reduce the heat to low. Let it simmer for about 1 to 1.5 hours, or until the beef is tender.
7. Once the beef is tender, add the cubed potatoes, sweet potato, plantain, and sliced chorizo to the pot. Simmer for another 10-15 minutes, or until the potatoes are fork-tender.
8. Add the quartered cabbage and bok choy to the pot. Cook until the vegetables are just tender but still crisp.
9. Season the Pochero with salt, pepper, and fish sauce or soy sauce to taste. Adjust the seasoning according to your preference.

10. Once the vegetables are cooked and the flavors have melded together, remove the pot from the heat.
11. Transfer the Pochero to a serving dish.
12. Garnish with chopped green onions or cilantro, if desired.
13. Serve hot with steamed rice.
14. Enjoy the hearty and comforting flavors of this Filipino Beef Stew!

Pochero is a versatile dish, and you can adjust the ingredients and seasoning according to your taste preferences. Feel free to add other vegetables such as carrots, green beans, or corn for added flavor and nutrition.

Rellenong Bangus (Stuffed Milkfish)

Ingredients:

- 1 large bangus (milkfish), scaled, gutted, and deboned
- 2 tablespoons cooking oil
- 3 cloves garlic, minced
- 1 onion, chopped
- 2 tomatoes, chopped
- 1 carrot, finely diced
- 1 bell pepper, finely diced
- 1 cup green peas (fresh or frozen)
- 3 tablespoons raisins
- 2 eggs, beaten
- Salt and pepper to taste
- Fish sauce (patis) or soy sauce, to taste
- Cooking twine or toothpicks
- Oil for frying

Instructions:

1. Preheat the oven to 350°F (175°C).
2. In a pan, heat the cooking oil over medium heat.
3. Add the minced garlic to the pan. Sauté until golden brown and fragrant.
4. Add the chopped onion to the pan. Sauté until the onion becomes translucent.
5. Stir in the chopped tomatoes and cook until they start to soften.
6. Add the finely diced carrot and bell pepper to the pan. Cook for a few minutes until the vegetables are slightly tender.
7. Mix in the green peas and raisins. Cook for another minute or two.
8. Season the vegetable mixture with salt, pepper, and fish sauce or soy sauce to taste. Adjust the seasoning according to your preference. Remove the pan from the heat and let the mixture cool slightly.
9. Meanwhile, prepare the deboned bangus by rinsing it under cold water and patting it dry with paper towels.
10. Stuff the bangus cavity with the cooked vegetable mixture, packing it in tightly.
11. Secure the opening of the bangus with cooking twine or toothpicks to hold the stuffing in place.

12. Brush the outside of the bangus with beaten eggs to help it brown during cooking.
13. Heat oil in a large pan over medium heat. Carefully place the stuffed bangus in the pan.
14. Fry the bangus on each side until golden brown, about 3-4 minutes per side.
15. Once browned, transfer the bangus to a baking dish and bake in the preheated oven for about 20-25 minutes, or until fully cooked through.
16. Once cooked, remove the bangus from the oven and let it cool slightly before slicing.
17. Serve the Rellenong Bangus slices with steamed rice and your favorite dipping sauce.
18. Enjoy the delicious and savory flavors of this classic Filipino dish!

Rellenong Bangus is perfect for special occasions or family gatherings and is sure to impress with its flavorful stuffing and beautiful presentation. Adjust the ingredients and seasoning according to your taste preferences.

Sinampalukang Manok (Chicken Tamarind Soup)

Ingredients:

- 1 whole chicken, cut into serving pieces
- 4 cups water
- 1 cup tamarind leaves and flowers (young tamarind leaves and flowers can be found in Filipino or Asian grocery stores)
- 2 medium-sized tomatoes, quartered
- 1 medium-sized onion, chopped
- 3 cloves garlic, minced
- 2 thumbs-sized ginger, sliced
- 2 long green chili peppers (siling pangsigang), sliced
- 1 cup spinach or kangkong (water spinach) leaves
- Fish sauce (patis) or salt, to taste
- Ground black pepper, to taste

Instructions:

1. In a pot, bring the water to a boil over medium heat.
2. Once boiling, add the chicken pieces to the pot. Let it simmer for about 15 minutes, skimming off any scum that rises to the surface.
3. Add the tamarind leaves and flowers to the pot. Continue simmering for another 10 minutes to allow the flavors to infuse.
4. Add the quartered tomatoes, chopped onion, minced garlic, and sliced ginger to the pot. Stir to combine.
5. Let the soup simmer for another 10-15 minutes, or until the chicken is fully cooked and tender.
6. Season the Sinampalukang Manok with fish sauce or salt and ground black pepper to taste. Adjust the seasoning according to your preference.
7. Add the sliced long green chili peppers to the pot. Let them simmer for a few more minutes to impart their flavor into the soup.
8. Add the spinach or kangkong leaves to the pot. Let them wilt in the soup for a minute or two.
9. Once the chicken is fully cooked, the vegetables are tender, and the flavors have melded together, remove the pot from the heat.
10. Transfer the Sinampalukang Manok to a serving bowl.

11. Serve hot with steamed rice.
12. Enjoy the tangy and flavorful taste of this traditional Filipino chicken tamarind soup!

Sinampalukang Manok is perfect for warming up on chilly days and is packed with refreshing sourness from the tamarind leaves and flowers. Feel free to adjust the ingredients and seasoning according to your taste preferences.

Adobong Pusit (Squid Adobo)

Ingredients:

- 1 lb (about 450g) squid (pusit), cleaned and sliced into rings
- 4 tablespoons soy sauce
- 4 tablespoons vinegar
- 4 cloves garlic, minced
- 1 onion, sliced
- 2 bay leaves
- 1 teaspoon whole peppercorns
- 2 tablespoons cooking oil
- Salt and pepper to taste
- Optional: sliced red chili peppers for extra heat
- Optional garnish: chopped green onions or cilantro

Instructions:

1. In a bowl, combine the soy sauce, vinegar, minced garlic, sliced onion, bay leaves, and whole peppercorns. Mix well to create the marinade.
2. Add the cleaned and sliced squid rings to the marinade. Toss to coat the squid evenly. Let it marinate for about 15-30 minutes.
3. Heat the cooking oil in a pan over medium heat.
4. Once the oil is hot, add the marinated squid (including the marinade) to the pan. Let it simmer for about 10-15 minutes, stirring occasionally, or until the squid is tender.
5. If desired, add sliced red chili peppers to the pan for extra heat.
6. Season the Adobong Pusit with salt and pepper to taste. Adjust the seasoning according to your preference.
7. Continue to simmer the Adobong Pusit until the sauce thickens slightly and coats the squid evenly.
8. Once the squid is tender and the sauce has thickened, remove the pan from the heat.
9. Transfer the Adobong Pusit to a serving dish.
10. Garnish with chopped green onions or cilantro, if desired.
11. Serve hot with steamed rice.
12. Enjoy the savory and tangy flavors of this classic Filipino Squid Adobo!

Adobong Pusit is best enjoyed fresh and pairs well with steamed rice or even with bread. Adjust the level of spiciness by adding more or fewer chili peppers. Feel free to customize the dish according to your taste preferences.

Kare-Kareng Gulay (Vegetable Stew in Peanut Sauce)

Ingredients:

- 2 tablespoons cooking oil
- 1 onion, chopped
- 4 cloves garlic, minced
- 2 cups sliced eggplant
- 1 cup sliced string beans (sitaw)
- 1 cup sliced banana heart (puso ng saging)
- 1 cup sliced bok choy (pechay)
- 1 cup sliced cabbage
- 1/2 cup ground roasted peanuts or peanut butter
- 4 cups vegetable broth or water
- 2 tablespoons annatto powder (atsuete) dissolved in 1/4 cup water
- Salt and pepper to taste
- Bagoong alamang (shrimp paste), for serving (optional)

Instructions:

1. Heat the cooking oil in a large pot over medium heat.
2. Add the chopped onion to the pot and sauté until translucent.
3. Add the minced garlic to the pot and cook until fragrant.
4. Stir in the sliced eggplant, string beans, and banana heart. Cook for a few minutes until slightly softened.
5. Pour the vegetable broth or water into the pot. Bring it to a boil, then reduce the heat to low and let it simmer for about 10 minutes, or until the vegetables are tender.
6. Add the sliced bok choy and cabbage to the pot. Cook for another 3-5 minutes, or until the leafy vegetables are wilted.
7. In a separate bowl, mix the ground roasted peanuts or peanut butter with the annatto water until well combined.
8. Pour the peanut mixture into the pot, stirring well to incorporate. Let the stew simmer for an additional 5-7 minutes to thicken the sauce.
9. Season the Kare-Kareng Gulay with salt and pepper to taste. Adjust the seasoning according to your preference.

10. Once the vegetables are tender and the sauce has thickened, remove the pot from the heat.
11. Transfer the Kare-Kareng Gulay to a serving dish.
12. Serve hot with steamed rice and bagoong alamang (shrimp paste) on the side, if desired.
13. Enjoy the rich and flavorful taste of this classic Filipino Vegetable Stew in Peanut Sauce!

Kare-Kareng Gulay is a comforting and satisfying dish that's perfect for vegetarians and those looking for meatless meal options. Feel free to customize the recipe by adding other vegetables of your choice, such as squash or okra. Adjust the thickness of the sauce by adding more or less peanut butter according to your preference.

Ukoy (Shrimp Fritters)

Ingredients:

- 1 cup small shrimps, peeled and deveined
- 1 cup bean sprouts (togue)
- 1/2 cup all-purpose flour
- 1/4 cup cornstarch
- 1/2 teaspoon baking powder
- 1/2 teaspoon salt
- 1/4 teaspoon ground black pepper
- 1/2 cup water
- 1 egg, beaten
- 1 small onion, thinly sliced
- 2-3 cloves garlic, minced
- Cooking oil for frying
- Vinegar dipping sauce (sukang sawsawan) or spicy vinegar, for serving

Instructions:

1. In a bowl, combine the all-purpose flour, cornstarch, baking powder, salt, and ground black pepper. Mix well.
2. Add the beaten egg and water to the dry ingredients. Stir until you have a smooth batter.
3. Add the peeled and deveined shrimps, bean sprouts, sliced onion, and minced garlic to the batter. Mix until the shrimps and vegetables are well-coated with the batter.
4. Heat cooking oil in a frying pan or skillet over medium heat.
5. Once the oil is hot, spoon the shrimp and vegetable mixture into the hot oil, forming small patties or fritters. Make sure to include some shrimps and vegetables in each spoonful.
6. Fry the Ukoy until golden brown and crispy, about 2-3 minutes per side.
7. Use a slotted spoon to transfer the cooked Ukoy to a plate lined with paper towels to drain excess oil.
8. Serve the Ukoy hot with vinegar dipping sauce or spicy vinegar on the side for dipping.
9. Enjoy the crispy and flavorful Ukoy as a snack or appetizer!

Ukoy is best enjoyed immediately while still hot and crispy. You can also customize this recipe by adding other ingredients such as shredded carrots or sweet potatoes for extra flavor and texture. Adjust the seasoning according to your taste preferences.

Pancit Bihon (Rice Noodles)

Ingredients:

- 250g rice noodles (bihon)
- 2 tablespoons cooking oil
- 2 cloves garlic, minced
- 1 onion, sliced
- 1 carrot, julienned
- 1 small cabbage, thinly sliced
- 1 red bell pepper, julienned
- 1 green bell pepper, julienned
- 1/2 cup sliced green beans
- 1/2 cup sliced snow peas (sitsaro)
- 200g cooked chicken breast, shredded (optional)
- 200g cooked shrimp, peeled and deveined (optional)
- 1/4 cup soy sauce
- 1/4 cup oyster sauce
- 4 cups chicken broth or water
- Salt and pepper to taste
- Calamansi or lemon wedges, for serving (optional)
- Chopped green onions or cilantro, for garnish (optional)
- Hard-boiled eggs, sliced, for serving (optional)

Instructions:

1. Soak the rice noodles (bihon) in warm water for about 10 minutes or until softened. Drain and set aside.
2. In a large pan or wok, heat the cooking oil over medium heat.
3. Add the minced garlic and sliced onion to the pan. Sauté until fragrant and the onion is translucent.
4. Add the julienned carrot, sliced cabbage, and julienned bell peppers to the pan. Stir-fry for a few minutes until the vegetables start to soften.
5. Add the sliced green beans and snow peas to the pan. Continue stir-frying for another 2-3 minutes.
6. If using cooked chicken breast or shrimp, add them to the pan and stir-fry until heated through.

7. Push the vegetables and meat to the side of the pan, creating a space in the center. Pour the soy sauce and oyster sauce into the center of the pan and stir to combine with the vegetables and meat.
8. Add the soaked rice noodles (bihon) to the pan. Gently toss to coat the noodles evenly with the sauce and distribute the vegetables and meat throughout.
9. Pour the chicken broth or water over the noodles. Allow the noodles to absorb the liquid and cook until tender, about 5-7 minutes, stirring occasionally.
10. Season the Pancit Bihon with salt and pepper to taste. Adjust the seasoning according to your preference.
11. Once the noodles are tender and most of the liquid has been absorbed, remove the pan from the heat.
12. Transfer the Pancit Bihon to a serving platter.
13. Garnish with chopped green onions or cilantro, if desired.
14. Serve hot with calamansi or lemon wedges on the side for squeezing over the noodles, and sliced hard-boiled eggs, if desired.
15. Enjoy the delicious and comforting flavors of this classic Filipino Pancit Bihon!

Gising-Gising (Spicy Green Beans in Coconut Milk)

Ingredients:

- 250g green beans, trimmed and sliced thinly
- 200g ground pork
- 1 tablespoon cooking oil
- 3 cloves garlic, minced
- 1 onion, chopped
- 2-3 pieces red chili peppers (siling labuyo), chopped (adjust according to your spice preference)
- 1 cup coconut milk
- Salt and pepper to taste

Instructions:

1. Heat the cooking oil in a pan over medium heat.
2. Add the minced garlic to the pan and sauté until fragrant.
3. Add the chopped onion to the pan and cook until softened.
4. Add the ground pork to the pan and cook until it starts to brown.
5. Once the pork is browned, add the chopped red chili peppers to the pan. Stir well to incorporate.
6. Add the sliced green beans to the pan and sauté for a few minutes until they start to soften.
7. Pour the coconut milk into the pan and bring it to a gentle simmer.
8. Let the mixture simmer for about 5-7 minutes, or until the green beans are cooked to your desired tenderness and the flavors have melded together.
9. Season the Gising-Gising with salt and pepper to taste. Adjust the seasoning according to your preference.
10. Once the green beans are cooked and the sauce has thickened slightly, remove the pan from the heat.
11. Transfer the Gising-Gising to a serving dish.
12. Serve hot with steamed rice.
13. Enjoy the spicy and creamy flavors of this delicious Filipino Gising-Gising!

Gising-Gising is best enjoyed immediately while still hot. Adjust the amount of chili peppers according to your spice tolerance. You can also add other vegetables such as carrots or bell peppers for added flavor and texture.

Ensaladang Talong (Eggplant Salad)

Ingredients:

- 2 large eggplants
- 2 medium tomatoes, sliced
- 1 small onion, thinly sliced
- 2 tablespoons vinegar (cane vinegar or white vinegar)
- 1 tablespoon soy sauce
- 1 tablespoon fish sauce (patis)
- 1 teaspoon sugar
- Salt and pepper to taste
- Chopped green onions or cilantro for garnish (optional)

Instructions:

1. Preheat your grill or oven to medium-high heat. If using an oven, you can also broil the eggplants.
2. Prick the eggplants with a fork or knife in several places to prevent them from bursting during cooking.
3. Grill or roast the eggplants until the skin is charred and the flesh is soft, turning occasionally to ensure even cooking. This usually takes about 15-20 minutes.
4. Once cooked, remove the eggplants from the grill or oven and let them cool slightly.
5. Peel off the charred skin from the eggplants and discard. Place the peeled eggplants on a serving plate or bowl.
6. Using a fork, gently mash the eggplants to flatten them slightly, but leave some texture.
7. Arrange the sliced tomatoes and onions on top of the mashed eggplants.
8. In a small bowl, whisk together the vinegar, soy sauce, fish sauce, sugar, salt, and pepper to make the dressing.
9. Drizzle the dressing over the eggplants, tomatoes, and onions.
10. Garnish with chopped green onions or cilantro, if desired.
11. Serve the Ensaladang Talong as a side dish or appetizer with grilled or fried fish, meat, or rice.
12. Enjoy the refreshing and tangy flavors of this classic Filipino Eggplant Salad!

Ensaladang Talong is a light and flavorful dish that's perfect for summer gatherings or as a refreshing side dish to complement your meals. Feel free to adjust the seasoning and add more ingredients according to your taste preferences.

Pork Menudo (Pork Stew)

Ingredients:

- 500 grams pork shoulder, diced into small pieces
- 200 grams pork liver, diced into small pieces
- 2 tablespoons cooking oil
- 3 cloves garlic, minced
- 1 onion, chopped
- 2 tomatoes, diced
- 2 potatoes, diced
- 1 carrot, diced
- 1 red bell pepper, diced
- 1 green bell pepper, diced
- 1 cup tomato sauce
- 1 cup water or pork broth
- 2 bay leaves
- 2 tablespoons soy sauce
- 1 tablespoon fish sauce (patis)
- Salt and pepper to taste
- 1/2 cup green peas (optional)
- 1/4 cup raisins (optional)
- Chopped green onions for garnish (optional)

Instructions:

1. Heat the cooking oil in a large pot over medium heat.
2. Sauté the minced garlic and chopped onion until fragrant and translucent.
3. Add the diced pork shoulder and pork liver to the pot. Cook until the pork is lightly browned on all sides.
4. Stir in the diced tomatoes and cook until softened.
5. Add the tomato sauce, water or pork broth, bay leaves, soy sauce, and fish sauce to the pot. Stir to combine.
6. Cover the pot and let the mixture simmer for about 30 minutes or until the pork is tender.
7. Add the diced potatoes, carrots, red bell pepper, and green bell pepper to the pot. Stir well.

8. Continue to simmer the stew for another 15-20 minutes or until the vegetables are cooked through.
9. If using, add the green peas and raisins to the pot and stir to incorporate.
10. Season the Pork Menudo with salt and pepper to taste.
11. Once everything is cooked and the flavors have melded together, remove the pot from the heat.
12. Transfer the Pork Menudo to a serving dish and garnish with chopped green onions, if desired.
13. Serve hot with steamed rice.

Enjoy the rich and hearty flavors of this Filipino Pork Menudo stew! Feel free to adjust the ingredients and seasonings according to your taste preferences.

Chicken Inasal (Grilled Chicken)

Ingredients:

Marinade:

- 1 kg chicken thighs or drumsticks
- 1/4 cup vinegar (cane vinegar or white vinegar)
- 1/4 cup calamansi juice or lemon juice
- 4 cloves garlic, minced
- 1 thumb-sized ginger, minced
- 2 stalks lemongrass, white part only, minced
- 2 tablespoons annatto oil or achuete oil
- 1 tablespoon soy sauce
- 1 tablespoon fish sauce (patis)
- 1 teaspoon ground black pepper
- 1 teaspoon sugar
- Salt, to taste

Dipping Sauce (optional):

- 1/4 cup vinegar
- 1/4 cup soy sauce
- 2 cloves garlic, minced
- 1-2 pieces bird's eye chili (optional)

Instructions:

1. In a bowl, combine all the marinade ingredients: vinegar, calamansi juice, minced garlic, minced ginger, minced lemongrass, annatto oil, soy sauce, fish sauce, ground black pepper, sugar, and salt. Mix well.
2. Place the chicken pieces in a large resealable plastic bag or shallow dish. Pour the marinade over the chicken, making sure each piece is well coated. Seal the bag or cover the dish with plastic wrap. Marinate in the refrigerator for at least 4 hours or overnight for best results.

3. Preheat your grill to medium-high heat. If using charcoal, make sure the coals are hot and glowing.
4. Remove the chicken from the marinade and let any excess drip off.
5. Grill the chicken pieces over medium-high heat, turning occasionally, until they are cooked through and have charred grill marks, about 20-25 minutes. Make sure the chicken is cooked to an internal temperature of 165°F (75°C).
6. While grilling, you can baste the chicken with the remaining marinade or annatto oil mixture to keep it moist and add more flavor.
7. Once the chicken is cooked, remove it from the grill and let it rest for a few minutes before serving.
8. Serve the Chicken Inasal hot with steamed rice and dipping sauce on the side, if desired.
9. To make the dipping sauce, simply combine vinegar, soy sauce, minced garlic, and bird's eye chili in a small bowl. Adjust the proportions according to your taste preference.
10. Enjoy the delicious flavors of Chicken Inasal!

Chicken Inasal is best enjoyed fresh off the grill, with its smoky and tangy flavors complementing the tender and juicy chicken.

Tinolang Tahong (Mussels Soup with Ginger)

Ingredients:

- 1 kg mussels (tahong), cleaned and debearded
- 2 tablespoons cooking oil
- 3 cloves garlic, minced
- 1 onion, sliced
- 1 thumb-sized ginger, sliced thinly
- 2 tomatoes, chopped
- 4 cups water or seafood broth
- 1 cup malunggay leaves (moringa leaves) or spinach
- Salt and pepper to taste
- Fish sauce (patis) or soy sauce for seasoning (optional)
- Calamansi or lemon wedges for serving (optional)

Instructions:

1. Heat the cooking oil in a pot over medium heat.
2. Sauté the minced garlic, sliced onion, and sliced ginger until fragrant.
3. Add the chopped tomatoes to the pot and cook until they start to soften.
4. Pour in the water or seafood broth and bring it to a simmer.
5. Once the broth is simmering, add the cleaned mussels to the pot. Cover and let them cook for about 5 minutes or until the mussels have opened.
6. Discard any unopened mussels.
7. Stir in the malunggay leaves or spinach and cook for another minute until wilted.
8. Season the Tinolang Tahong with salt and pepper to taste. You can also add fish sauce or soy sauce for additional seasoning if desired.
9. Once everything is cooked and seasoned to your liking, remove the pot from the heat.
10. Ladle the Tinolang Tahong into bowls and serve hot.
11. Serve with calamansi or lemon wedges on the side for squeezing over the soup, if desired.
12. Enjoy the warm and comforting flavors of this Filipino Tinolang Tahong soup!

Tinolang Tahong is best enjoyed fresh and hot, with its delicate broth infused with the flavors of ginger and seafood. Feel free to adjust the ingredients and seasonings according to your taste preferences.

Ginataang Manok (Chicken in Coconut Milk)

Ingredients:

- 1 kg chicken pieces (thighs, drumsticks, or breast), cut into serving pieces
- 2 tablespoons cooking oil
- 3 cloves garlic, minced
- 1 onion, chopped
- 1 thumb-sized ginger, sliced thinly
- 2-3 pieces green chili peppers (siling haba), sliced (optional)
- 2 cups coconut milk
- 1 cup water or chicken broth
- 1 cup spinach or kangkong (water spinach) leaves, washed and trimmed
- Fish sauce (patis) or salt to taste
- Ground black pepper to taste

Instructions:

1. Heat the cooking oil in a large pot or deep skillet over medium heat.
2. Sauté the minced garlic, chopped onion, and sliced ginger until fragrant and the onion is translucent.
3. Add the chicken pieces to the pot and cook until they are lightly browned on all sides.
4. If using, add the sliced green chili peppers to the pot and sauté for a minute to release their flavor (adjust the amount according to your preferred level of spiciness).
5. Pour in the coconut milk and water or chicken broth. Stir to combine.
6. Bring the mixture to a simmer, then lower the heat and let it gently simmer for about 20-25 minutes, or until the chicken is cooked through and tender. Stir occasionally.
7. Once the chicken is cooked, add the spinach or kangkong leaves to the pot. Stir and let them wilt into the sauce.
8. Season the Ginataang Manok with fish sauce (patis) or salt and ground black pepper to taste. Adjust the seasoning according to your preference.
9. Let the dish simmer for another 2-3 minutes to allow the flavors to meld together.
10. Once everything is cooked and seasoned to your liking, remove the pot from the heat.

11. Transfer the Ginataang Manok to a serving dish.
12. Serve hot with steamed rice.
13. Enjoy the rich and creamy flavors of this Filipino Chicken in Coconut Milk dish!

Ginataang Manok is best enjoyed fresh and hot, with its creamy sauce coating the tender chicken pieces. Feel free to customize the recipe by adding other vegetables such as squash or string beans for added flavor and texture.